One Period | Global Developments | Side by Side

THE ANCIENT WORLD

4500-500 BCE

Alex Woolf

Illustrated by Victor Beuren

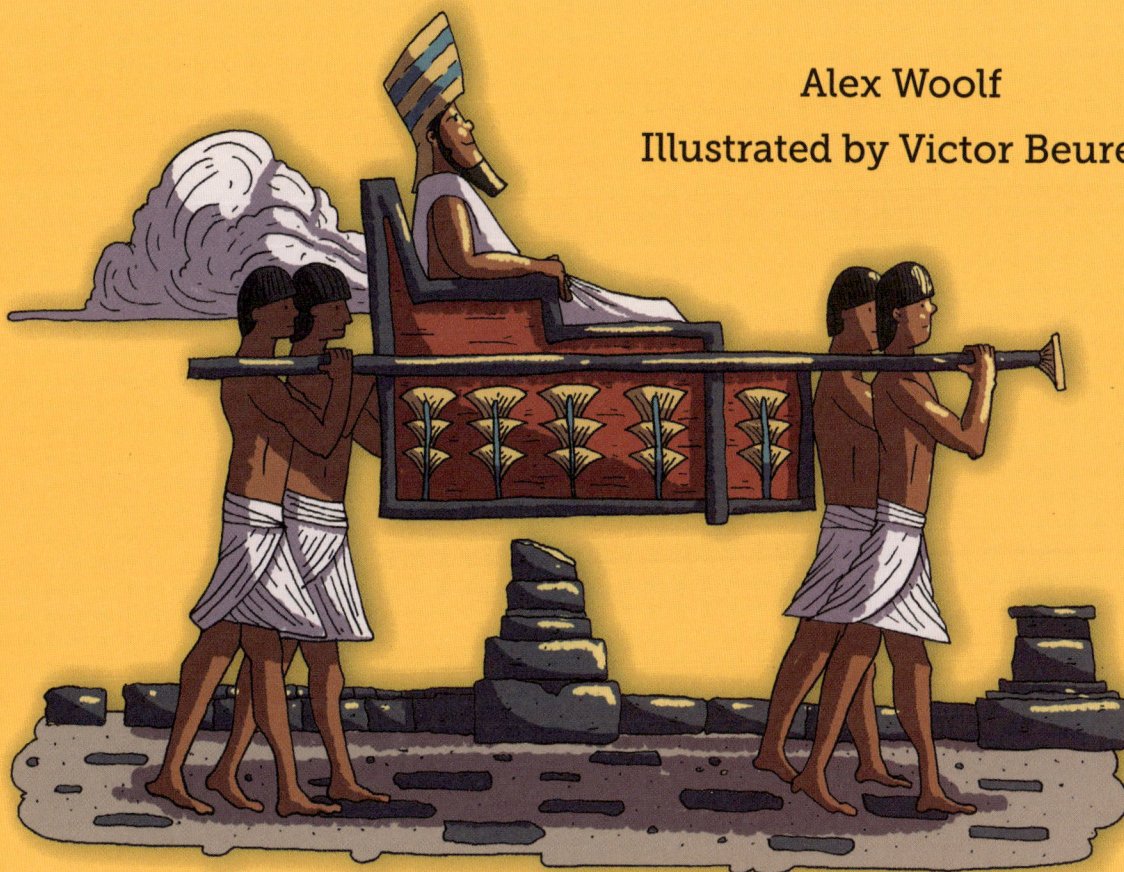

W

FRANKLIN WATTS

LONDON·SYDNEY

Franklin Watts
First published in Great Britain in 2017
by The Watts Publishing Group

All rights reserved.

Credits
Artwork by Victor Beuren
Design: Collaborate Agency
Editor: Nicola Edwards

ISBN 978 1 4451 5701 6

Printed in China

Franklin Watts
An imprint of
Hachette Children's Group
Part of The Watts Publishing Group
Carmelite House
50 Victoria Embankment
London EC4Y 0DZ

An Hachette UK Company
www.hachette.co.uk

www.franklinwatts.co.uk

❉ CONTENTS ❉

❖ INTRODUCTION ❖

What we now call the ancient world began with the dawn of civilisation. Before then, humans lived in simple farming communities or as nomadic tribes. Starting from about 4500 BCE, people began building the first cities ruled over by kings. Laws were issued. Money was invented, allowing trade to flourish. The first writing systems were developed. This was the start of history. The ancient world ended with the dawn of the classical era, in about 500 BCE.

Colour Key
- Africa
- Americas
- Asia
- Europe
- Australia and Oceania

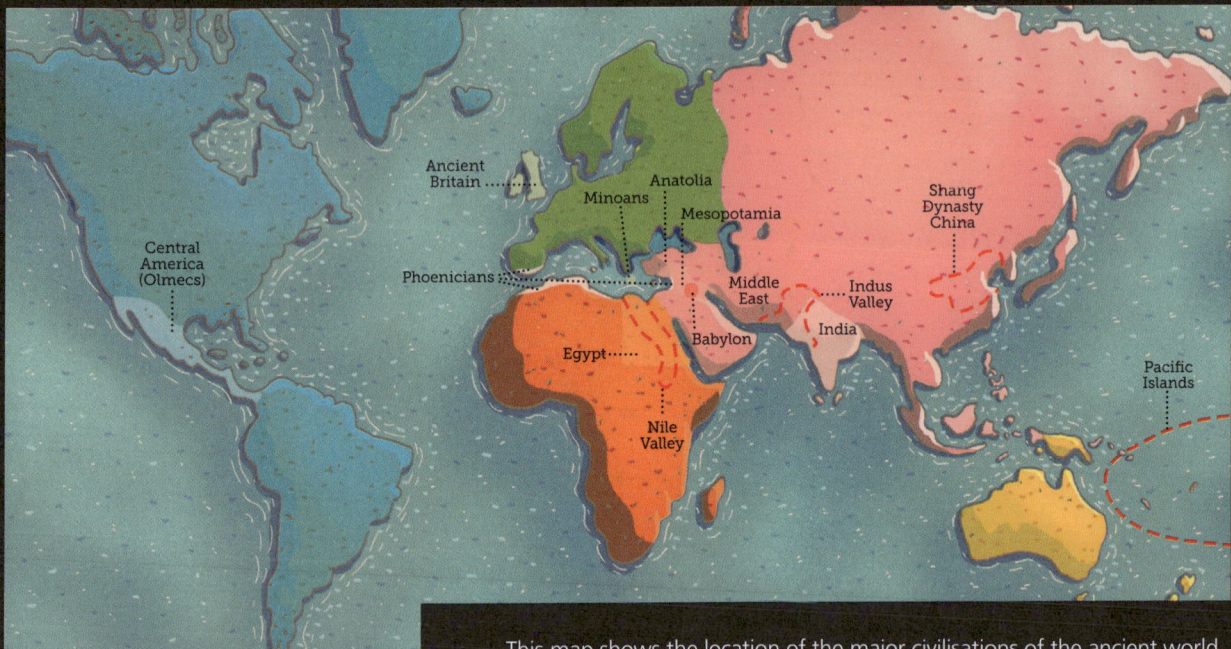

Central America (Olmecs)

Ancient Britain

Minoans

Anatolia

Mesopotamia

Shang Dynasty China

Phoenicians

Middle East

Indus Valley

Egypt

Babylon

India

Nile Valley

Pacific Islands

This map shows the location of the major civilisations of the ancient world.

Where it began

Civilisation first arose in Mesopotamia, where Iraq is located today. On the fertile floodplains between the Tigris and Euphrates rivers, farmers were able to grow more than they needed. They could sell their produce. This freed people to do other jobs. They could become warriors, merchants and priests. Rulers ordered the construction of roads, canals, temples and palaces.

The Mesopotamians built great stepped towers called ziggurats.

Civilisation spreads

In other fertile parts of the world, where farmers were able to produce a surplus of crops, other civilisations emerged. In about 3300 BCE, the first kings rose to power in the Nile Valley of Egypt. In 3100 BCE, towns started to appear in the Indus Valley of north-west India. Over the next 600 years, kingdoms were established on the Mediterranean island of Crete and in China.

The earliest known writing dates from around 3300 BCE in the Mesopotamian city of Uruk. Today, scholars call this form of writing cuneiform.

The people of the Indus Valley built elaborate cities with their own water supply and sanitation systems.

Writing

As civilisations grew more complex, administrators, merchants and traders could no longer store all the information they needed in their heads, and systems of writing became necessary. Writing began as pictures to represent objects or ideas. Later, cultures developed signs to represent words, then the sounds of speech – creating the first alphabets.

A wall painting shows the pharaoh Ramesses II (1279–1213 BCE) in battle against the Nubians.

War

Before the arrival of civilisation, tribes often fought each other over land and possessions. But it was with the building of the first cities that war in the modern sense began. Cities fortified themselves against enemy attack, and states fought each other with armies.

❈ GOVERNMENT AND POLITICS ❈

In the ancient world, a person's position in society was most commonly decided by their birth. Kings were born into this role, usually as the eldest male of the most powerful family. They built themselves fine palaces and their deeds were glorified in art and poetry. At first, kings tended to be both religious and military leaders. Later, the religious role passed on to priests.

China

The Shang dynasty of kings dominated China from 1766 to 1122 BCE. The kings had teams of officials to help them rule and collect taxes. From 1122 to 771 BCE, China was ruled by the Zhou. Zhou kings developed the 'Mandate of Heaven'. This was a 'god-given' right to rule, so long as they were just. Unjust kings could be overthrown.

King Tang was the first king of the Shang dynasty.

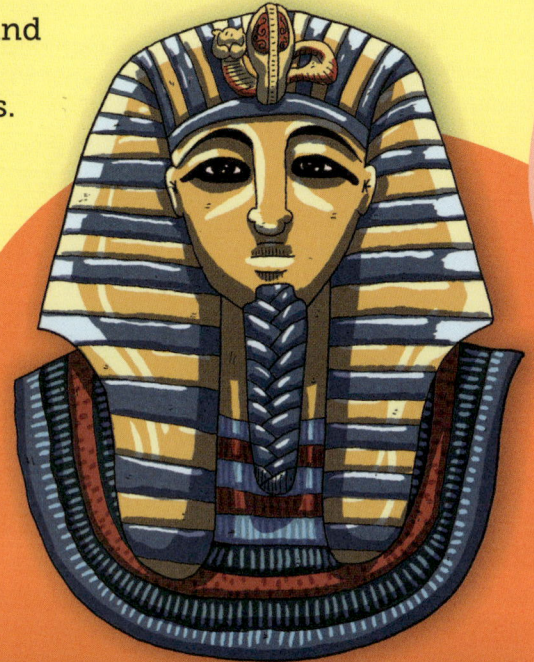

Pharaohs were said to be chosen by the gods to rule, and were regarded as gods in human form. This is the mask of the pharaoh Tutankhamun.

Egypt

The kings of ancient Egypt were called pharaohs. They were in charge of the government, the army and the law. They were helped by thousands of administrators, the most important of which was the vizier. He was in charge of the nomarchs – heads of Egypt's 42 districts.

C. 2925 BCE Narmer becomes the first pharaoh of all Egypt

India

The Indus Valley civilisation collapsed in about 1700 BCE. Some two hundred years later, a Central Asian people called the Aryans began to settle in India. By 900 BCE, the Aryans had formed a number of kingdoms ruled over by rajas (kings) with the help of Brahmins (priests).

Under the Aryans, society became divided into hereditary castes (classes) with the Brahmins and Kshatriya (nobles) at the top.

Mesopotamia

Ancient Mesopotamia suffered frequent floods, ruining harvests. The chief role of Mesopotamian kings was to maintain adequate food stores and to distribute these in times of flood. Kings were also lawgivers, imposing harsh punishments on those who disobeyed them. Mesopotamian kings performed regular sacrifices to the gods to stave off natural disasters.

Mesopotamian kings built temples to honour the gods.

2334 BCE First great empire in history founded in Mesopotamia by Sargon of Akkad	**1344 BCE** Akhenaten changes Egypt's religion from worship of many gods to one god, Aten
1813 BCE Assyrians under Shamshi-Adad become major power in Mesopotamia	
1787 BCE Babylonia under Hammurabi takes control of Mesopotamia	**1122 BCE** Cruel Shang king Di-xin overthrown by Wu of Zhou, who establishes Zhou dynasty

2000 BCE .... **1500 BCE** .... **1000 BCE** .... **500 BCE**

FOOD AND FARMING

Most people in the ancient world were farmers. For successful farming, people had to learn how to water the land by digging artificial channels. This process, known as irrigation, allowed crops to be grown even during dry spells. The most important crops included cereals, such as wheat, barley, millet, oats and rice, as well as fruit and vegetables.

In Egypt, reapers cut the ripe corn with wooden sickles edged with sharp flints.

Mesopotamian irrigation canals carried water to desert areas, allowing more food to be produced.

Egypt

In the fertile soil of the Nile Valley, many crops were grown, including wheat for bread and beer, and vegetables such as leeks, onions, garlic, beans and lettuce. For dessert, the Egyptians ate small round cakes, or fruit such as melons and figs. They sweetened their food with honey and dates. There was little land for grazing, so meat was an expensive luxury.

Mesopotamia

Mesopotamia's rivers flooded at the wrong time, when crops were already growing, so flood water had to be channelled and stored for later use. The most important food crops were barley and dates. Mesopotamian farmers also grew onions, melons, cucumbers and figs.

c. 7000 BCE Wheat and barley cultivated in Mesopotamia

c. 8000 BCE Squash first cultivated in Mexico

c. 5000s BCE Rice and millet cultivated in China

c. 3000 BCE First ox-drawn ploughs in Egypt

c. 3000 BCE Egyptian farmers start growing vines for wine

4500 BCE   4000 BCE   3500 BCE   3000 BCE

Central America

In Mexico, a people called the Olmecs flourished between 1300 and 400 BCE. Olmec lands were prone to flooding, making their soil very fertile. They grew maize, beans, chillies, tomatoes and squashes, and kept dogs and chickens for meat. They also hunted deer, wild pigs, turtles and alligators.

China

As early as 5000 BCE, millet and rice were cultivated in China. Rice must be grown on level ground in flooded fields, called paddies. Chinese farmers brought more land under cultivation by cutting sloping hillsides into terraces, or steps.

ARCHITECTURE

With civilisation came the emergence of towns and cities. People needed different kinds of buildings: houses, workshops, storage places, temples and palaces. In hot countries, people built with sun-dried mud bricks. In cooler regions, they built with clay, mud, wicker, wood and stone.

Thousands of workers helped build the pyramids, many of them slaves or prisoners.

Some 5,000 people lived in Çatalhöyük in 1,000 houses.

Egypt

The Egyptians built enormous stone pyramids as tombs for their pharaohs. The first was built in steps. Later ones were smooth-sided. The biggest is the Great Pyramid, which took 20 years to build and was made from 2.3 million blocks.

Workers used rollers to move the blocks, and may have used wooden levers to lift them into place.

Çatalhöyük

The settlement of Çatalhöyük in Anatolia, which flourished between 6500 and 5500 BCE, had an unusual architecture. There were no streets. The houses were linked to each other like cells in a beehive. People climbed down ladders from flat rooftops to get into their homes.

Imhotep, earliest known architect, built first Egyptian pyramid — c. 2650 BCE

c. 8000 BCE — Jericho built in Palestine – one of earliest known settlements

Skara Brae

In about 2500 BCE, the village of Skara Brae was built in Orkney, off the north coast of Scotland. There was no wood on the island, so people built everything with stone – even the furniture. The harsh winds forced them to build into the ground for shelter. Low, covered passages led from one dwelling to another. There was a drain from each of the houses leading to a common sewer.

Inside each of the Skara Brae dwellings there was a large, square room with a fireplace in the middle.

The cities of the Indus Valley contained dockyards, granaries, warehouses and public baths.

Indus Valley

The Indus Valley cities of Mohenjo Daro and Harappa had houses with sewers, wells and baths. Many of the larger houses had two stories, with several rooms built around an open courtyard. The cities were surrounded by massive defensive walls.

c. 2050 BCE Ziggurat of Ur built in Mesopotamia

c. 1250 BCE Olmecs built the first American pyramids

2500s BCE Pyramids of Giza built in Egypt, including Great Pyramid

c. 1500 BCE Palace of Minos built in Knossos, Crete

c. 1900s BCE Temple of Karnak, largest temple in Egypt

2000 BCE .... 1500 BCE .... 1000 BCE .... 500 BCE

WAR AND CONFLICT

Early ancient armies used the same weapons that had been wielded in conflict since prehistoric times: slings, bows and arrows, wooden spears and clubs. Stone was often bound to wood to give extra weight and sharpness. From 3700 BCE, the first metal weapons were used. The use of chariots and, later, cavalry (horsemen), gave armies speed of movement.

Assyria

The Mesopotamian power of Assyria rose to dominance in about 2300 BCE under Sargon of Akkad, who created one of the earliest standing armies. The key weapon of the Assyrian army was the chariot, used as a mobile command or fighting platform, for battlefield communications and to smash into enemy formations.

Assyrian chariots were drawn by two or more horses. From 2000 BCE, the chariots had spoked wheels, making them lighter and faster.

Egypt

Egyptian infantry (foot soldiers) carried spears and shields, and were supported in battle by archers. Starting in 1600 BCE, new military technologies began to be used, including horse-drawn chariots, sickle swords and cast bronze body armour. Part-time farmer-soldiers were replaced by professional warriors.

Egyptian soldiers used a hooked bronze weapon called a khopesh, or sickle sword.

Horse-drawn war chariots are used in Sumer — c. 2500 BCE

c. 3000 BCE — Earliest depictions of siege warfare found in Egyptian tomb reliefs

4500 BCE ⋯⋯⋯⋯ 4000 BCE ⋯⋯⋯⋯ 3500 BCE ⋯⋯⋯⋯ 3000 BCE

Shang soldiers carried spears, poleaxes, dagger-axes and bows and arrows.

China

Shang infantry wore helmets made of bronze or leather and were armed with stone and bronze weapons. The Shang king kept a personal army at his capital, and he would lead his soldiers into battle. Chariots were used in China from about 1200 BCE. The Shang used them as mobile command platforms, but not for fighting.

India

The Aryan kingdoms frequently fought with each other. They used bronze weapons and horse-drawn, spoke-wheeled chariots, and sometimes war elephants. Warriors belonged to a caste (class) of nobles called the Kshatriya. The raja (king) would personally lead them into battle.

The Battle of Kurukshetra, described in the Indian epic *Mahabharata*.

2400s BCE Copper daggers used in Minoan Crete

1100s BCE Iron starts to replace bronze in weapon-making

1600s BCE Bronze swords used in Minoan Crete

c. 1000 BCE Assyrians are first to use cavalry effectively

1210 BCE First known sea battle occurs when Hittites defeat a fleet from Cyprus

800s BCE Earliest recorded use of warriors on horseback in Central Asia

2000 BCE .... 1500 BCE .... 1000 BCE .... 500 BCE

☀ SCIENCE AND TECHNOLOGY ☀

In ancient times, people studied the way the world worked in order to try and improve their lives. Their observations of the heavens, together with their understanding of mathematics, helped them create the first calendars. By experimenting with materials they were able to make better tools, weapons and buildings. They invented machines – levers, wheels and pulleys – to lift and move heavy objects.

In the Indus Valley, clay was used to make cookware, pottery and sculptures.

The Mesopotamians were expert astronomers, making accurate predictions of lunar eclipses, and the movement of the planets and stars.

Indus Valley

The people of the Indus Valley invented buttons made from shells by around 2000 BCE. These were used as ornaments at that time, rather than as fasteners. They also had accurate measuring devices, including weights and rulers, and made tools of flint, copper and bronze, such as hammers, needles, fish-hooks, axes, razors and saws.

Mesopotamia

The Mesopotamians invented the wheel in about 3500 BCE, used at first for making pottery, and later for chariots. They had a wide knowledge of geometry and mathematics, using a number system based on 60, and were able to perform complex multiplication and division.

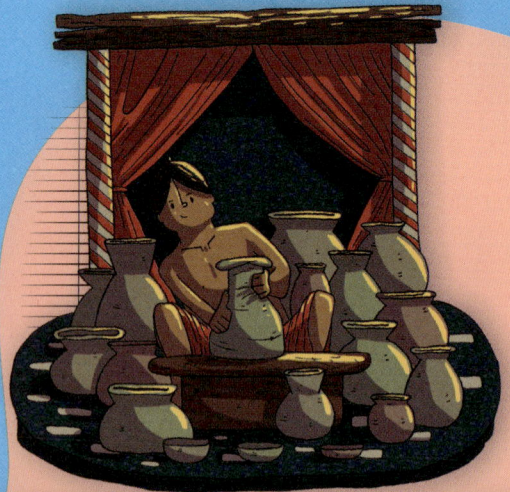

Egyptian number-hieroglyphs suggest mathematical calculations — c. 3250 BCE

3000 BCE — Chinese are using a 365-day calendar

Egyptians are using irrigation channels to water their fields — 3100 BCE

Egypt

The Egyptians used devices such as wedges, levers and pulleys to build their pyramids. They invented papyrus, a form of paper, built sailing ships and lighthouses, and discovered sophisticated ways for mummifying or embalming dead bodies. In medicine, they understood the functions of internal organs and could identify diseases. They lanced boils and set broken bones.

The Shang made beautifully worked tools and weapons from bronze.

China

The Shang observed the movements of the Sun, Moon and stars to develop a calendar with a 360-day year, based on the solar and lunar cycles. They were also skilled mathematicians with a decimal number system involving odd and even numbers.

1400 BCE   Indians are using the shadoof to raise water from rivers or lakes

TRANSPORTATION

The first form of transport was, of course, walking. When people learned to domesticate animals – donkeys, horses, oxen and camels – they began using them for transport. With the invention of the wheel came animal-drawn vehicles. Tracks were widened into roads, enabling long-distance trade and communication. The earliest boats were dug-out canoes or rafts of logs lashed together with vines.

An ancient Chinese ox-drawn cart.

The Lapita travelled in boats made from two dug-out canoes lashed together with plant fibre.

China

There is no evidence that wheeled transport existed in China before the arrival of the chariot in about 1200 BCE. From around this time, they began attaching harnesses to horses and oxen so they could pull covered carts carrying heavy loads of farm produce. All Shang cities were sited on rivers, and boats and rafts were another important form of transport.

South-East Asia

The Lapita people travelled vast distances across the Pacific Ocean. In about 1500 BCE, they set out from their South-East Asian homeland in their canoes. Propelling themselves with paddles or small sails, they navigated by the Sun, the stars, currents and swells. By 900 BCE, they had colonised many Pacific islands, including Fiji, Tonga and Samoa.

7600 BCE | Earliest known dug-out canoes found in the Netherlands

Domestication of camel in Somalia and southern Asia | c. 3000 BCE

Phoenician warships had two banks of oars, for speed and manoeuvrability in battle.

Phoenicians

The Phoenicians, based in present-day Lebanon, achieved a mastery of seafaring that led them to dominate the Mediterranean from around 1100 to 600 BCE. They built single-masted wooden trading ships, and warships with a battering ram at the bow, or front end. The Phoenicians discovered how to navigate using the North Star, and may have sailed around Africa and as far as the Azores and Britain.

Egypt

High-status Egyptians would be carried in litters – chairs with poles attached, carried by slaves. Apart from horse-drawn chariots, wheeled vehicles were rarely used. Heavy loads were placed on sledges and dragged by teams of men. Donkeys and mules were used as beasts of burden.

In ancient Egypt, litters were used to transport pharaohs during processions and religious ceremonies.

✦✦ ART AND LITERATURE ✦✦

It was rare for ancient peoples to make beautiful objects for the enjoyment of others. Art was often created for religious or political purposes, to honour the gods, or to glorify kings and celebrate military victories. Literature emerged out of traditional stories and songs. For centuries, these were told or sung from memory. With the invention of writing systems, they were written down.

The legendary King of Uruk, Gilgamesh, battles with monsters in his quest for everlasting life.

In Egyptian tombs, a draughtsman first drew an outline of the picture over a grid of squares, then a painter coloured it.

Mesopotamia

Mesopotamian artists created clay cylinder seals, statuettes and relief carvings, showing scenes of animals, deities and kings. The Assyrians produced colossal guardian figures – lions or winged beasts with human heads. The Mesopotamian *Epic of Gilgamesh* is regarded as the earliest surviving great work of literature.

Egypt

Ancient Egyptian art included paintings, stone and ceramic sculpture, jewellery, and drawings on papyrus. Styles of art changed very little over 3,000 years of history. Representations of people were stylised rather than realistic. In tomb paintings, colours had meanings. White stood for joy; red for blood and life; green for water and new life; black for fertility.

c. 3100 BCE   Egyptians start to paint walls of tombs

4000s BCE   Sumerians in Mesopotamia make jewellery and painted pottery

Minoans

The Minoans of Crete, who flourished from 3650 to 1400 BCE, excelled at art. They produced colourful frescoes, stone carvings and carved seal stones. Minoan pottery depicted sea creatures, birds, flowers and animals, as well as abstract lines and patterns. They also created elaborate jewellery – diadems (jewelled crowns or headbands), necklaces, bracelets and beads – using gold, silver, bronze and semi-precious stones.

A Minoan fresco showing bull-leaping, a ritual connected with bull worship in which a person would make an acrobatic leap over a bull.

Olmecs

The Olmecs of ancient Mexico produced a variety of sculptures and figurines, from strange, mythical creatures to surprisingly realistic human figures. They worked in jade, clay, basalt and greenstone. They are most famous for their carvings of enormous helmeted heads.

Some of the colossal Olmec heads are up to 3.4 metres high.

✳ CHILDREN AND EDUCATION ✳

In ancient times, many infants died during childbirth, so the birth of a healthy child was a cause for celebration. Usually, only the children – and often only the sons – of the rich and privileged went to school. For children of poor families, childhood was short. As soon as they were old enough, they were expected to help their parents in their work.

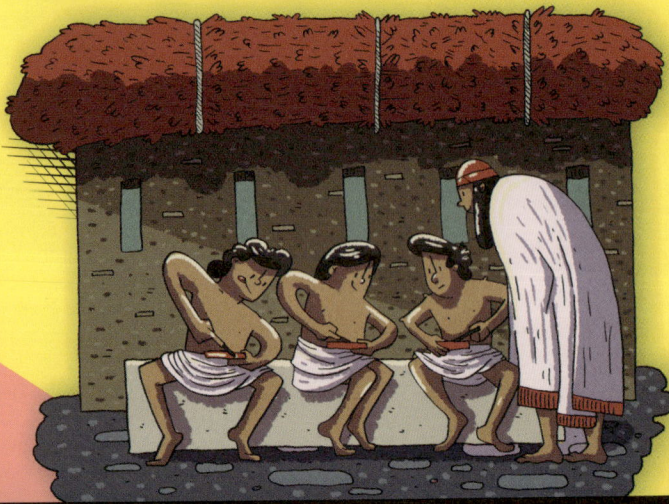

The main subjects Egyptian children learned were reading, handwriting and arithmetic.

During morning lessons, Mesopotamian boys did writing exercises.

Mesopotamia

In Mesopotamia, most boys were taught their father's trade or were apprenticed to learn a trade. Girls stayed home with their mothers to learn housekeeping skills and help look after younger children. Sons of wealthy and professional people went to schools run by priests. They were taught reading, writing, mathematics, medicine, law and astrology.

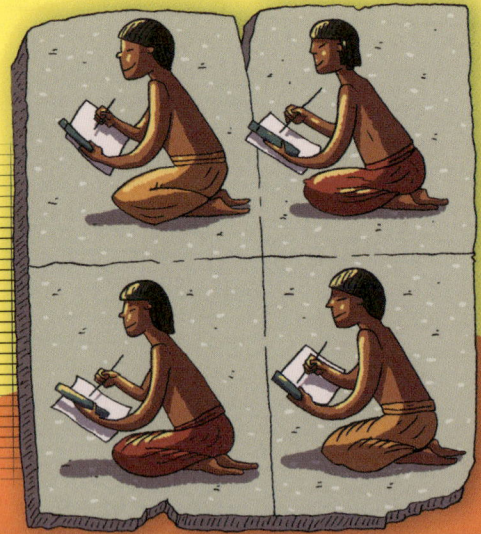

Egypt

Poor Egyptian children learned to do their parents' jobs. Farmers' children, for example, helped with the sowing and harvesting. They began their working lives as young as five. Trainee priests and scribes began their education between the ages of five and ten. They were given punishments including beatings and copying out stories.

c. 3000 BCE

Excavated tablets from this time record details of school life in

Children of farming families in China helped their parents work the land.

China

During the Zhou Dynasty, which began in 1122 BCE, five national schools were set up for the education of noble children. Boys were taught the 'Six Arts'. These were ritual, music, archery, charioteering, calligraphy (decorative handwriting) and mathematics. Boys who excelled in these arts were considered perfect gentlemen. Girls were taught ritual, correct deportment (way of standing and walking), silk making and weaving.

Gurukula were ancient Indian schools where pupils would live with, or near, the guru (teacher).

India

In ancient India during the period of the Aryan kingdoms, most education was based on the *Vedas*, a collection of religious poems. Children were taught how to pronounce and recite the Veda. They also learned about nature, logic, medicine and practical knowledge. As the caste (class) system became stricter, only sons of Brahmins (priests) and Kshatriya (nobles) were allowed access to education.

2000 BCE — Toddlers in the Indus Valley were playing with toy carts pulled by miniature bulls

2300s BCE — *The Instruction of Ptahhotep,* an Egyptian book for teachers

1500s BCE — Estimated start of education in China

The followers of Chinese philosopher Confucius spread his ideas, influencing Chinese education — *300s BCE*

2000 BCE   1500 BCE   1000 BCE   500 BCE

CRIME AND PUNISHMENT

As ancient peoples began to form into large, settled communities, laws were needed to maintain order. Punishments for breaking the laws generally had two aims: to exact revenge for the damage done, and to deter others from carrying out similar crimes. Early societies often wrote down their laws in collections called codes.

Moses and his tablets of law. The most famous of these laws are the Ten Commandments.

King Hammurabi of Babylonia had his 282 laws inscribed on stones and clay tablets.

Hebrews

Moses was a Hebrew prophet and lawgiver living in around 1300 BCE. His code, known as Mosaic Law, is found in the Old Testament of the Bible and consists of 613 laws. Some of these laws are harsh, for example one says that anyone who sacrifices to another god is to be killed. The Mosaic code continued the Babylonian idea of revenge – an eye for an eye, a tooth for a tooth.

Babylon

The Code of Hammurabi, a king of Babylon, proclaimed the principle of retaliation – a life for a life. So murder was punished by death, but so were other crimes. These included lying, stealing from a temple and mixing with known criminals. Those found guilty might be drowned, stoned, hanged or beheaded.

Hittites

The Hittite Empire, which was based in Anatolia (modern Turkey) in the 1000s BCE, had a different approach to punishment. Instead of revenge, it asked for restitution – making good a wrong. So for killing in anger, the price was four slaves given to the victim's family. For breaking an arm or leg, the price was 20 silver coins, called shekels.

The Hittites punished criminals by making them pay money to non-royal victims. Mutilation – for example, the amputation of limbs – was reserved for people who had offended the king.

Egypt

Egyptian laws were written by the pharaoh, and punishments were administered by the vizier (see page 6). Those who plotted against the pharaoh were punished with impalement – a very slow, painful death. For tomb raiding, the punishment was beheading or drowning. For vandalising temples, people could be burned alive. For minor (or petty) crimes, such as stealing, tax evasion and illegal trading, punishments included beatings, amputation and imprisonment.

Petty criminals in ancient Egypt often received beatings with a cane.

c. 2100 BCE	Code of Ur-Nammu in Mesopotamia, the oldest surviving law code
c. 1650 BCE	Hittite law code
c. 1750 BCE	Code of Hammurabi
c. 1300 BCE	Mosaic Law
c. 621 BCE	Draco, a lawmaker in Greece, issues a code punishing almost every crime with death
c. 1075 BCE	Assyrian law code, similar to the Code of Hammurabi, but with harsher punishments

2000 BCE   1500 BCE   1000 BCE   500 BCE

LEISURE AND ENTERTAINMENT

Long before written records began, people of all cultures enjoyed sports and entertainment. In the ruins of ancient civilisations, archaeologists have found musical instruments, toys and games. Wall paintings show scenes of wrestling and other combat sports. Such contests may have helped improve fighting and survival skills.

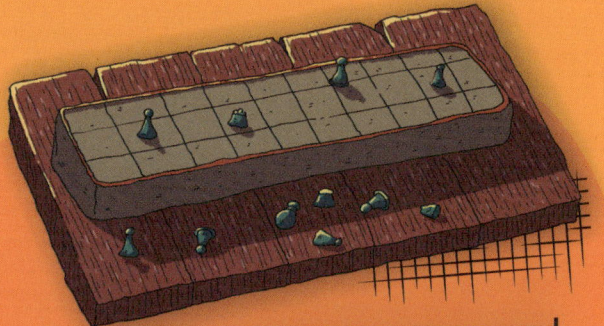

The most popular board game in ancient Egypt was *Senet* – the 'game of passing', something like the modern game of backgammon.

For a Mesopotamian ruler, a successful lion hunt was a sign he enjoyed the gods' favour.

Egypt

Ancient Egyptians indulged in many sports, including wrestling, boxing, stick fighting, archery, hunting and chariot racing. Fishermen would joust with each other on water, pushing other boats away with long poles. Tomb paintings show children playing leap frog and tug-of-war, and racing each other. Egyptians also loved music. They played flutes, pipes, lyres, harps, drums and rattles.

Mesopotamia

Mesopotamian kings spent their leisure time hunting fierce animals such as lions. During religious festivals, banquets were held where guests were entertained by musicians, jugglers, acrobats and snake charmers. Epic poems were recited about gods and famous battles. Board games with counters and dice, such as the Royal Game of Ur, were popular. Children played with boomerangs, bows and arrows, spinning tops and rattles.

c. 3000 BCE

Paintings in Egyptian tombs show scenes of handball

Clay models of a cart like this one may have been played with by an Indus Valley child.

India

The people of the Indus Valley held regular sporting competitions involving weapons including the *toran* (javelin) and *chakra* (discus). Children played with toy carts, whistles shaped like birds, and toy monkeys that could slide down a string. The Aryans raced chariots, played fighting games and loved to tell stories.

The Shang invented *cuju*, said to be the oldest football game in the world.

China

Music was very important in ancient Chinese society. Instruments included bronze cymbals, drums, gongs, chimes and bells. Musicians also played *xuns* (egg-shaped ceramic wind instruments). Theatrical entertainments were put on involving music, clowning and acrobatics. Children played with a *da tuoluo* – a colourful spinning top, spun by a whip.

2500 BCE	Regular sporting contests held in Indus Valley	
c. 2300 BCE	Oldest known dice game excavated from Mesopotamian tomb	**1160** BCE Earliest known sporting event: a wrestling contest between Egyptian and foreign soldiers
c. 2000 BCE	Minoans develop the sport of bull-leaping	**776** BCE The first Olympic Games is held in Greece

2000 BCE .... 1500 BCE .... 1000 BCE .... 500 BCE

❋ RELIGION ❋

Religion may have begun as a search for a meaning to life. By worshipping natural forces, early humans may have hoped the Sun would keep rising and their crops would continue to grow. By 4000 BCE, the idea of supernatural beings controlling the world had taken root. Powerful kings and priests claimed to act with the authority of these gods. This led to the first organised religions.

Egypt

The Egyptians had many deities – perhaps up to 2,000 of them. Many of these were local gods, worshipped by a town, village or even one family. There were also powerful deities (see right) that everyone worshipped. Temples were built to honour them.

Powerful Egyptian gods included (left to right) Osiris, Ra, Isis, Horus, Throth and Anubis.

Ancient Britain

The ancient Britons built hundreds of stone circles, which played an important part in their religious life. The most famous of these is Stonehenge in Wiltshire, built between 3000 and 1500 BCE. The ancient Britons believed that the Sun and Moon had a special power over their lives. It's likely that they held ceremonies at Stonehenge on Midsummer's Day (the longest day of the year) and Midwinter's Day (the shortest day of the year).

Stonehenge may have been in continuous use as a centre of religious ceremonies for around 2,000 years.

c. 3500 BCE People in the Mediterranean and Mesopotamia are worshipping mother goddesses

Final stage of construction of Stonehenge c. 2600 BCE

India

The Aryans worshipped
many gods who they
believed could offer them
good things, such as victory
in war, health, wealth and
heroic sons. Important gods
included Indra, Agni, Mitra
and Varuna. To win their
favour, Brahmins recited
religious poems called the
Vedas (see page 21).

Hebrews

The Hebrews, later known as the Jews,
emerged in the Middle East in the
1000s BCE. Though never a military
power, they made a profound impact
on history due to their belief in one
God, which would lead to the founding
of three great religions. Their early
history was a struggle: they were
enslaved or conquered by the
Egyptians, Assyrians and Babylonians.
Yet they held fast to their beliefs.

According to the Bible, Moses parted the Red Sea as
he led the Hebrews out of slavery in Egypt to freedom.

c. 2400 BCE *Pyramid Texts*, the oldest surviving religious
texts, are composed in Egypt

c. 1300 BCE Possible date of Moses and Exodus from Egypt

c. 1500 BCE Amun-Ra becomes the main Egyptian god

c. 1700 BCE The *Vedas* (Aryan religious poems) start to be composed

DEATH AND BURIAL

Rituals surrounded death even among early humans. The oldest graves yet discovered were found in China and date back 400,000 years. Neanderthals living in Europe and Asia tens of thousands of years ago buried their dead in the caves they lived in, together with valued possessions and food, suggesting they believed that life continued after death.

The Mesopotamian underworld was guarded by scorpion people, with the upper body of a man and the tail of a scorpion.

In ancient Egypt an embalmed body was wrapped in bandages to make a mummy.

Mesopotamia

The Mesopotamians believed that everyone, good or bad, faced the same sad fate: the dead went to live in a gloomy underworld, or 'land of no return'. The underworld was inside a mountain. The dead ate dust and clay and wore wings instead of clothes. Mesopotamian kings were buried in huge underground tombs surrounded by their belongings. Their servants were killed and buried with them.

Egypt

The Egyptians had a much happier view of the afterlife. They believed good people went to live forever in the kingdom of Osiris, which was like a perfect version of Egypt. Embalmers preserved the corpses, removing the organs, then drying out the bodies. They placed them in a sarcophagus, together with their most precious possessions, and sealed them up in a tomb.

27,000 BCE — Earliest grave yet found in Europe – the 'Red Lady of Wales' – dates from this time

5000 BCE — In Banpo, China, villagers buried in individual graves with possessions and tools

4500 BCE — Sumerians in Mesopotamia bury their dead with food and tools

China

The Shang believed the souls of the dead lived in the nether world (a place under the earth), and graves were their earthly residences. The royal family had vast, elaborate tombs filled with treasures, as well as the corpses of servants and sacrificed prisoners.

The Shang worshipped their ancestors and believed that through this they stayed involved in earthly matters.

The Aryans believed cremation prevented dead spirits from remaining among the living.

India

The Aryans cremated their dead. Agni, god of fire, was responsible for transporting the souls of the dead to heaven. Later, Brahmins began to embrace the idea of reincarnation (rebirth). They claimed the only way to escape the endless cycle of death and rebirth was to achieve *moksha*, or self-knowledge, by overcoming ignorance and desire.

GLOSSARY

abstract
Describes art that does not show reality, but takes the form of shapes, colours and textures.

astrology
The study of the movements and positions of the Sun, Moon, stars and planets in the belief that these things influence human affairs.

beasts of burden
Animals that are used for carrying goods.

c.
Stands for 'circa' and means approximately or about.

ceramic
Made of clay and permanently hardened by heat.

chariot
A two-wheeled vehicle drawn by horses, used in ancient times for racing and warfare.

colonise
Settle an area and establish control over it.

cremation
The disposal of a dead person's body by burning it to ashes, usually after a funeral ceremony.

deity
A god or goddess.

draughtsman
A person who makes detailed plans or drawings.

dynasty
People from the same family who succeed each other as rulers of a country or empire.

eclipse
The obscuring of the light of a celestial body (such as the Sun) by the passage of another (such as the Moon) between it and the observer.

embalming
Preserving a corpse from decay.

floodplain
An area of low-lying ground next to a river. The land is formed mainly from fertile river sediments and is subject to regular flooding.

fresco
A painting done on wet plaster on a wall or ceiling. The colours penetrate the plaster and become fixed as it dries.

granary
A storehouse for grain.

hereditary
Describing a system in which a title or right is passed down from parent to child.

hieroglyphs
Pictures that represent words, syllables or sounds. Hieroglyphs are used in some early writing systems.

irrigation
The supply of water to farmland, usually by the digging of channels.

joust
Engage in a sporting contest, usually on horseback, in which opponents fight with lances or poles.

lyre
A stringed instrument like a small, U-shaped harp, used especially in ancient Greece.

manoeuvrability
The ability to be moved around easily while in motion.

nomadic
Describes the life of nomads, people who travel from place to place to find fresh pasture for their animals.

papyrus
Paper-like material produced in ancient Egypt from the stem of a water plant, and used for writing or painting on.

poleaxe
A short-handled axe with a spike in the back.

pulley
A wheel with a grooved rim around which a cord passes, used to raise heavy weights.

relief carving
A carving in which the design stands out from a surface.

retaliation
Harming someone because they have caused harm – an act of revenge.

sacrifice
An act of slaughtering an animal or surrendering a possession as an offering to a deity.

sarcophagus
A stone coffin, often adorned with a sculpture or inscription.

sewer
An underground channel for carrying off drainage water and waste matter.

shadoof
A pole with a bucket and a counterbalancing weight, used for raising water.

sickle
A short-handled farming tool with a curved blade.

sling
A strap or loop used as a simple weapon, to hurl stones or other small missiles.

standing army
A permanent army that is composed of full-time, professional soldiers.

steppe
A large area of flat, unforested grassland in South-East Europe or Central Asia.

stylised
Depicted in an exaggerated or non-realistic style.

surplus
An excess of produce.

wicker
Pliable twigs, typically of willow, plaited or woven to make walls or items such as furniture or baskets.

ziggurat
A rectangular stepped tower found in ancient Mesopotamia.

FURTHER INFORMATION

Books

Ancient China (Explore!)
Izzi Howell
Wayland, 2016

Ancient Egypt (The History Detective Investigates)
Rachel Minay
Wayland, 2015

Daily Life in the Indus Valley
Brian Williams
Raintree, 2016

Sumer and Ancient Mesopotamia (Technology in the Ancient World)
Charlie Samuels
Franklin Watts, 2015

Websites

Find information and resources on Mesopotamia here:
www.mesopotamia.co.uk

Discover all about ancient Egypt here:
discoveringegypt.com

A useful resource on ancient China:
www.ancientchina.co.uk

Explore the people, culture, beliefs and history of ancient India here:
www.ancientindia.co.uk

Learn about ancient African history here:
www.pbs.org/wonders

INDEX